my itty-bitty bio

Malala Yousafzai

Published in the United States of America by Cherry Lake Publishing
Ann Arbor, Michigan
www.cherrylakepublishing.com

Reading Adviser: Marla Conn, MS, Ed, Literacy Specialist, Read-Ability, Inc.
Book Designer: Jennifer Wahl
Illustrator: Jeff Bane

Photo Credits: © Shahid Khan/Shutterstock.com, 5; © Patrick Poendl / Shutterstock.com, 7; ©DFID – UK Department for International Development/Flickr, 9, 21; © Kdonmuang/Shutterstock.com, 11; ©Southbank Centre/ Flickr, 13; © tutae/Shutterstock.com, 15; © trabantos/Shutterstock.com, 17, 22; © Bair175/Wikimedia, 19, 23; Cover, 1, 6, 10, 18; Various frames throughout, ©Shutterstock Images

Library of Congress Cataloging-in-Publication Data

Names: Spiller, Sara, author. | Bane, Jeff, 1957- illustrator.
Title: Malala Yousafzai / Sara Spiller ; illustrated by Jeff Bane.
Description: Ann Arbor, Michigan : Cherry Lake Publishing, 2019. | Series: My itty-bitty bio | Includes bibliographical references and index.
Identifiers: LCCN 2018034511| ISBN 9781534142718 (hardcover) | ISBN 9781534140479 (pdf) | ISBN 9781534139275 (pbk.) | ISBN 9781534141674 (hosted ebook)
Subjects: LCSH: Yousafzai, Malala, 1997---Juvenile literature. | Girls--Education--Pakistan--Juvenile literature. | Girls--Violence against--Pakistan--Juvenile literature. | Women social reformers--Pakistan--Biography--Juvenile literature. | Taliban--Juvenile literature. | Pakistan--Social conditions--Juvenile literature.
Classification: LCC LC2330 .S65 2019 | DDC 371.822095491--dc23
LC record available at https://lccn.loc.gov/2018034511

Printed in the United States of America
Corporate Graphics

table of contents

My Story 4

Timeline 22

Glossary 24

Index 24

About the author: Sara Spiller is a native of the state of Michigan. She enjoys reading comic books and hanging out with her cats.

About the illustrator: Jeff Bane and his two business partners own a studio along the American River in Folsom, California, home of the 1849 Gold Rush. When Jeff's not sketching or illustrating for clients, he's either swimming or kayaking in the river to relax.

I was born in Pakistan.

It was 1997.

Education was important to my parents. It still is. My father led schools.

My mother could not read. But she wanted me to go to school.

What is important to your parents?

There is a group called the **Taliban**. Its members do not like schools for girls. They **attacked** these schools.

I told people that girls should have an education.

I began **blogging**. I used a fake name.

Why would someone use a fake name?

Many people listened to me.
I won a **prize** for my work.
The Taliban did not like this.

They wanted to hurt me.
A man came on my school bus.
He shot me. I was 15.

But I survived. I was sent to England. I finished my high school education in England.

I won the Nobel Peace Prize in 2014. This goes to people who do important work.

I started an all-girl school for **Syrian refugees** on my 18th birthday.

I returned to Pakistan in 2018. I had not been back home since I was shot.

I still fight for women's education. I talk to people all over the world!

What would you like to ask me?

timeline

2012

1990

Born
1997

2014

2090

glossary & index

glossary

attacked (uh-TAKD) to have hurt someone or something

blogging (BLAWG-ing) writing on a web page or website to talk about something

education (ej-uh-KAY-shuhn) the process of teaching and learning

prize (PRIZE) something you get for winning

Syrian refugees (SEER-ee-uhn ref-yoo-JEES) people from the country of Syria who were forced to leave their country to escape the war

Taliban (TAHL-ih-bahn) a group that wants to force people to follow strict rules of a religion called Islam

index

blogging, 10

education, 6, 10, 16, 20

England, 16

fake name, 10, 11

Nobel Peace, 18

school, 6, 8, 14, 16
- all-girl, 8, 20
- Syrian refugees, 20

Taliban, 8, 12